MW00613984

IN THE CLOUDS

Published by Hellgate Press

(An imprint of L&R Publishing, LLC)

Hellgate Press

PO Box 3531

Ashland, OR 97520

email: sales@hellgatepress.com

Interior & Cover Design: L. Redding

ISBN: 978-1-954163-30-0

Printed and bound in the United States of America

First edition 10 9 8 7 6 5 4 3 2 1

IN THE CLOUDS

Voices of Pr'Line Mountain, Vietnam: 1970-1971 ... and Now

ROBERT L. MENZ, ET AL.

Hellgate Press   Ashland, Oregon

This book is dedicated to our adult children
Strong, Caring, Giving and Blended
From our oldest to our youngest

Ruth's oldest son David and our daughter-in-law Kim
Robert's daughter Gwen and our son-in-law Todd
Ruth's youngest son Matt
Robert's son Shawn and our daughter-in-law Cathy
Three decades ago, two became one

This is also dedicated to our six grandchildren
Hannah, Jeffrey, Madie, Sofia, Hailey and Gracie
We are Blessed!

CONTENTS

INTRODUCTION

~I WON IN VIETNAM~

It was cold in January when I swore the "oath."
Colder was Ft. Leonardwood where I learned "dagger and cloak."
Extreme "makeover" was the temp and place —
The Central Highlands of Vietnam wore a different "face."
The "World," oh the world, we longed to see.
"Memories" of breakfast, hot showers, and iced tea.
I learned that rats were tasty, "fish oil" wasn't for vets,
Monsoons wreaked havoc, and loneliness was "wet."
More than the sun there could "fry" your skin.
Cobras and "3 steppers" were close and within.
Mosquitoes exchanged "fluids" with us during the night —
We were filled with "poison," some oozed with fright.
I was shot at and missed a time or "three."
"To thee and to thee, but not unto me."

Blasts took my dinner and my "balance" away.
The "sounds of silence" in my left ear will stay.
After one full year and a day and a "half,"
It was 1971, and I completed my "lap."
I finished the course – my "war" was over.
My God — my God, "Red Rover, Red Rover."
So, my "return," unlike many others,
"58000" of my sisters and brothers,
Calls for a "life" that now must count.
Grace I've felt in an "infinite" amount.

That which was experienced — lost "innocence" and pain,
For me, turned into a "kaleidoscope" of gain.
An "agape" friend who would die for me,
A lifestyle to cherish, and the freedom to "be."
Emotions in "Nam" ran very high
And to scale this span was to "know" alive.
"Broken" bones heal the strongest and perhaps inner ears too,
But it was my "Spirit" that expanded to a place all new.
When I returned to "riots" and experienced a calm,
I knew I "won" in Vietnam.
There still are wars and rumors with "spins" —
Wars raging "without," yet a sanctuary within. (RLM)

* * * *

THIS BOOK REPRESENTS STORIES and narrative experiences from veterans who served on Pr'Line Mountain, Vietnam, during the time frame of 1970/1971. Many served on the mountain before and after that snapshot in time, and I'm sure their stories would be equally meaningful. The reason for focusing on this period results from the reconnecting, after about fifty years, of those who served during this time.

Mike Brogan and I stayed in touch after we were discharged from the army. Mike is from Massachusetts, and I was first in Missouri and now live in Ohio. We were in each other's homes on many occasions. We learned later that others in our group also stay connected.

Several years ago, when Mike and his wife Rosie were visiting my wife Ruth and me, we talked about some of the others we had served with and wondered how and

Pr'Line Mountain in the clouds

where they were. Of the names we were collectively able to remember, I set out to find them with my limited knowledge of the world wide web. Through various means, I was able to locate two of my old friends who were deceased. The wife of one seemed appreciative and interested in our efforts. Later I was able to connect with Marc Bourque from Maine. Like most of us who get unsolicited calls from strangers, he let it go to voicemail. Marc, Mike and I roomed together most of our time on Pr'Line. When Marc heard my voice and message, he called back immediately.

Next, I tried to call Ken Ottens. Ken had extended his tour of duty and spent more time on Pr'Line than most of us. I found several Ken Ottens, yet found one who was the same age as I am and was from Illinois, as I remembered Ken was.

"Hello."

"Hello my name is Bob Menz, and I'm trying to find the Ken Ottens who served on Pr'Line Mountain, Vietnam."

"What year?"

I knew it was him! As it turned out, Ken went back to Pr'Line in the early 1990s, thus the question, "What year?" One month after the initial phone call, we met in a hotel at a halfway spot. After nearly fifty years, we picked up where we left off! Ken's wife Janice and my wife Ruth were amazed at our recollection of stories and experiences over our two-day reunion.

Here's where it gets interesting. Ken and Janice exerted great effort into finding the others with whom we served. As with me, Ken heard many times, "sorry you have the wrong person." But because of their persistence, the Ottens have located virtually everyone in our company that served on Pr'Line Mountain in 1970/1971. About ten of the thirty-five we have located are deceased. Several are not doing well. The rest of us are chugging along for a bunch of guys in their seventies.

On Veteran's day 2019, five of us had a reunion in Ohio. Wow the stories we resurrected! Since then, through the initiative of Mike and Rosie, we "zoom" on the last Sunday evening of the month. As of this writing, our next big reunion is delayed because of the COVID 19 virus.

There were about sixteen of us who served in the signal corps on Pr'Line at any one point in time. Because our tours were staggered, we knew those who came before and left after our given tours. My tour of duty was from September, 1970, to September, 1971. I was a "newbie" to those who arrived in January of 1970, and I was an "old timer" to those who arrived in June of 1971. Thus, the timeframe of 1970/1971.

Tropo section of Pr'Line with our equipment and hooches

Below is a list of my brothers who have contributed to this book. Through our tours of duty, we indeed became brothers. This is the ethos that permeates this book. We skipped the ritual of joining cut fingers, but we became blood brothers. I did not realize until we all reunited, how much I love these guys.

Marc Bourque: Marc served with the Tropo brotherhood on Pr'Line Mountain, Vietnam, from January, 1971, to November, 1971. He and Patricia have been married for forty-six years and live in Kennebunkport, Maine. They have two children, a son and a daughter. Sadly, their son passed away over twenty years ago. They enjoy spending time with their only grandson. Marc retired from the Portsmouth Naval Shipyard as a production shop planner after thirty-five years of government service. After his retirement, he worked part time at several jobs just to keep busy. When Marc fully retired, he and Patricia volunteered at the local food pantry two to three days a week. Marc enjoys gardening and starts his own flowers in early February for summer planting around their house. Marc and Patricia now plan to travel and see this beautiful country.

Mike Brogan: Mike served with the Tropo brotherhood on Pr'Line Mountain, Vietnam, from September, 1970, to September, 1971. He and Rosemary are approaching their fiftieth wedding anniversary. They have three sons and one daughter and are proud grandparents of nine, ranging in ages from nineteen years to twenty-two months. Rosie received an associate's degree as a Medical Secretary and Mike received an Advanced Electronics Certificate from a local technical school. In their early years they both worked in their fields. Later, after being sidelined by their kids, they worked in different disciplines for several years. Mike finally settled in for his last twenty-six working years as Buildings and Grounds Maintenance Supervisor, (the most challenging and fun working years). Now that they have retired, they are enjoying family, travel and some fun part time jobs.

Ken Ottens: Alias "OTT" or best known as "Water boy." He served with the Tropo brotherhood on Pr'Line Mountain, Vietnam, from January, 1970, to July, 1971 (one year, six months and two days). He and his wife, Janice, live in Fulton, Illinois. They have two daughters. Ken eased into the working world in the electrical trade and after an intense training period of five years, became a Journeyman Wireman Electrician with the IBEW. Ken was also a volunteer fireman for fourteen years. He attended extra classes to earn more firefighting skills and application of those skills. Janice worked as a Registered Dietitian. In 1983, Ken had a chance to go to the Philippines and work on a project at a school in rural Cavite Province. In 1992 Ken, Janice and their girls moved to the school to work on various projects at the school and surrounding area for over two years. While in the Philippines, Ken had the opportunity to go to Vietnam. The main reason was to look at the possibility of starting an orphanage and clearly to return to Pr'Line Mountain and Dalat. He did make the side trip to visit his home "in the clouds." The North Vietnamese had taken control of the former site and was still using it to send out signals. Ken is now retired, but continues to enjoy numerous projects in his "Man Cave" garage.

Jerry Sharp: Jerry served with the Tropo brotherhood on Pr'Line Mountain, Vietnam, from January, 1971, to November, 1971. He and Dolores (Dee) live in Newman Lake, Washington. They have two sons, both of whom are married. They have six grandchildren and one great granddaughter. Jerry spent his working days in the sawmill profession and retired from Idaho Veneer Co. in 2010, as Plant Superintendent. Dee spent her working days as a jewelry salesperson. Jerry and Dee love to travel and spend time with family in the southern states. Jerry Loves to hunt, and both Dee and Jerry love to fish.

Jim Singleterry: Jim served with the Tropo brotherhood on Pr'Line Mountain, Vietnam, from January, 1970, to January, 1971. He and Shari live in Harrisburg, Oregon. Together they have three grown children and six grandchildren. They also have various informally adopted grandchildren and some great grandchildren beyond count. After his time in the army, Jim worked for the State of Oregon on a forestry crew then decided to get a job that was not subject to the weather. To satisfy his lifelong curiosity about how things work, Jim went to a community college to learn diesel mechanics. He now has time to putter in his shop making and fixing things and enjoys reading after his retirement as a mechanic for thirty-seven years.

Jim (Tex) Thomas: Jim served with the Tropo brotherhood on Pr'Line Mountain, Vietnam, from January, 1970, to January, 1971. After returning stateside, he served another year at Fort Monmouth, then he and Martha went home to Texas. Jim worked as a title company escrow officer overseeing real estate transactions for nearly forty years then spent another four years as a title consultant for a consulting engineering firm building highways and toll roads for the State of Texas. These days, Jim keeps up with his rental properties and three grandchildren who live about ninety miles from he and Martha. In 2018, Jim and Martha celebrated fifty years of marriage.

Len Weir: Len served with the Tropo brotherhood on Pr'-Line Mountain, Vietnam, from February, 1970, to February, 1971. He and Ann live in Oakland, Pennsylvania, a suburb of Pittsburg. They have three daughters and eight grand-

Equipment in one of the Tropospheric Scatter Microwave Communication vans

children ranging in ages from two to twenty-one. Len spent twenty-eight years as a customer service manager for a large computer company. Prior to full retirement, Len and Ann lived in southwest Florida for fifteen years where Len worked in retail management. After retiring, they returned to Pittsburg in 2014, to spend more time with their expanding family.

My heartfelt thanks to these contributors. The stories of these men will be in italics.

1

ARRIVAL

~SENSELESS~

Nam had days too bland to savor.
Yet we tasted.
The essence of our surroundings could distort olfaction.
Yet we smelled.
The melodious noise orchestrated discord.
Yet we heard.
The panoramic scene was a frequent spectacle.
Yet we saw.
The emotional paralysis was novel.
Indeed, we were ofttimes numb. (RLM)

* * * *

S ILENCE.
Dead silence.
Touchdown. More silence. Beep of the intercom.
"This is your captain, welcome to Cam Ranh Bay. Gentlemen, I tried to get you here before midnight where yesterday would have counted for the first day of your tour. I'm sorry we missed it by minutes. On behalf of all of us at Tiger Airlines, we wish you all safety and health."

My mind was in a cloud. Defensiveness assured me that Vietnam could not be as bad as I read that it was or saw that it was on the TV news. It was the end of August, 1970, and I was a strong, albeit skinny, twenty-one-year-old. *I will survive this*, I thought. "I will be OK," I prayed.

After deplaning, we spent hours on the tarmac filling out paperwork before the sun rose. When forms were filled out in triplicate, and we walked toward a barracks in the daylight, I saw dozens of Vietnamese women walking hitherto. All were dressed in black stove-legged slacks and large cone-shaped hats, conical hats, called in native tongue, *no n la*. They were wearing the same hats I had seen on the news many times before. *Oh my God*, it occurred to me, *this is really how they dress*. The TV news was not creating drama! This was real! *Oh no*, I thought, *could the catastrophic reports of war be real too*? I wasn't sure about the other "newbies" in my group, but I felt perplexed. I was exhausted. I was in a cloud.

Brogan: *After graduating with my 26L20 MOS from Fort Monmouth, Uncle Sam asked me to suggest three places that I would like to be stationed. Looking for adventure, I wrote down that my first choice was to be stationed in the tropics of the Republic of Vietnam. Uncle was glad to accommodate my choice.*

When I finally landed in Nha Trang, after flying for twenty-one hours, my excitement was peaked. As I stepped out of the Tiger Airlines air-conditioned jet, the extreme heat seemed to suck the air out of my lungs. In the distance, mortars could be heard. "This was my choice! What was I thinking?"

As was often the case in the military, we hurried and then we waited. Upon arrival, while the sun was asleep and my energy eclipsed, we addressed forms. Then for over a week, I waited to learn what I was to do in this country, and where, exactly, I was to go. I did my AIT (advance individual training) at Fort Monmouth, New Jersey. Fort Monmouth was the United States Army Signal School and a plush setting to gain my military occupational specialty (MOS). Students there were trained in installation, maintenance, operations, and repair of complex communications and cryptographic equipment. Training there was two to four times longer than most AIT's, and most of the "students" there had volunteered into the army and requested this MOS. Even though I was drafted, I had tested high enough in electrical, electronics and technology skills that the army decided it was worth the further investment in my training at Fort Monmouth. My father was an electrician, and I did not appreciate how much of his knowledge had rubbed off and blessed me. Further, I cannot begin to enumerate the many other ways that my dad blessed me, my siblings and my mother. While many troops were training to fight and shoot, I was in a classroom learning about ohms, amps, circuits and the like.

But back to my waiting in Cam Ranh. I grew more anxious day by day. I was told that I would be sent where I was needed. Being assigned to an infantry company was not out of the question. This kind of assignment would have been outside my training but not "out of the question." There was the right way, the wrong way, and the Army way! Clarity was often partly cloudy because many decision makers had their heads in the clouds!

Alas my orders came through, and I was assigned to the 362nd Signal Company on Pr'Line Mountain. Pr'Line (pronounced "praline," short for primary line and so named from being the primary signal site in South Vietnam) was a signal site on the second highest mountain in South Vietnam and peeked out of the impenetrable jungles of the Central Highlands. I had heard of and had seen pictures of Pr'Line Mountain before, as some of my instructors at Fort Monmouth had served on Pr'Line. It was these pictures that first revealed the carpet of white clouds below the perimeter of the berm. And now I was on my way to what was to be, for the next year, my home "In the Clouds."

It was an amazing journey as we convoyed through small villages and hamlets. The ascent from the South China Sea revealed lower temperatures as we traversed over eighteen-hundred meters in elevation, yet it exposed a higher risk of ambush as Highway 1 penetrated the dense vegetation. The canopy of trees and vines turned the mid-day sun into twilight. Also being revealed as we moved into the Central Highlands (that was not evident on the coast) was a horrid smell. The smell of rotten, putrid unfiltered stink. This must be, I concluded, the colon of the earth. I looked down over the cliffs and traverses that our convoy had just traveled as we climbed higher and higher. The tiny road where we had trekked just minutes earlier, was just a ribbon of hair-pinned turns. This was not the colon of the earth, I mused. This tubular corridor was too small. These loopbacks must be the facsimile of the duodenum, Jejunum and the Ileum. This was some twenty-two kilometers of mucosal folds that emptied into what I hoped would be relief. As for now, however, I only experienced anxiety. This

Climbing into the Central Highlands toward Pr'Line Mountain

concentration of olfactory sensation was to become the fragrance of Vietnam. The striking beauty of the Central Highlands, was at times, very ugly.

Four of us in this convoy wore new fatigues. Two were headed to Lang Biang Mountain (LBM) which was a sister signal site to Pr'Line. LBM was about thirty kilometers further down the road and about ten kilometers as the chopper flew. Each mountain was visible to the other. Two of us, Mike and I, were to hop off the deuce-and-a-half (2 ½ ton truck) train at Pr'Line.

> **Singleterry**: *I left Seattle in January. After a brief stopover in bitter cold Alaska, I was on my way to Vietnam. I had not mentally prepared myself for the cold, which one would normally associate with*

Alaska wintertime, because my thoughts were on adapting to the heat and jungles of Nam. After arriving in Vietnam, we were directed from the plane to a bus where windows were covered in heavy metal mesh. I could not figure out if that was to keep us in a cage and to keep us from escaping, or to keep out the bad guys – either way it felt like a bad situation. As a result, I was scared spitless and didn't have a bowel movement for three days.

My first experience riding a deuce-and-a-half was my transit up the Central Highlands to eventually get to Pr'Line. I expected to be riding with a bunch of other GIs, however, I found that the civilian Vietnamese often utilized our trucks to get from place to place. A girl about ten or twelve years of age climbed aboard and smiled. I didn't speak the language, but I figured I should smile back. She asked me if I wanted to go boom boom. Still not knowing what she was talking about, I smiled and said yes. A more experienced soldier beside me said she wanted to know if I wanted sex. I didn't want to be involved in this behavior and resolved, then and there, to be wary of what I said before agreeing to anything.

Bourque: *After arriving in Cam Ranh, we were directed to a covered deuce-and-a-half where we rode in a small convoy for the long ride to Nha Trang. I worried that we were going to get "hit" because no one on my truck had been issued a weapon. When we finally arrived at the base in*

Nha Trang, we filled out paperwork, got shots and were issued M-16 rifles. I found it strange that after being supplied my weapon and several clips of ammunition, I was not given a chance to site my weapon on a firing range. But then again, I was in the Signal Corps and felt hopeful that I would never have to use it. After several days, Randy and I were assigned to our duty station, Pr'Line Mountain. We first flew from Nha Trang to Dalat in a small cargo plane. The landing was bumpy as heck - like landing on a washboard.

Until now I had not been in a true Vietnamese environment. There were very few military personnel around us at the Dalat Airport, unlike what we had experienced for the past week, which was wall-to-wall military protection. Then there was the language barrier. I had no clue what was being said by the local inhabitants, and there was no way to tell who was friend or foe. From there we took an armored personnel carrier (APC) and rode to our rendezvous spot in Dalat. The APC had no windows and it was like riding in the dark for what seemed like an hour. When we finally stopped, we found ourselves in front of a large white building and were told that this was Ann's House. This, I was later to learn, was a common checkpoint. We were advised to stay near the APC because we would shortly join a convoy from there to Pr'Line Mountain.

After waiting a few minutes, a young Vietnamese girl, about ten years old, came by and asked, "GI

Church in Dalat did not escape the damage of war

want Coke?" Randy and I looked at each other and thought a Coke would be nice, and I asked, "How much?" She replied, "Price $5.00." We were both shocked at the asking price and replied at the same time, "that is too much." She responded by saying, "Number one very best Coke." She then pulled two small green plastic containers from her pocket. This is when we realized she was selling drugs and not a soft drink. No wonder so many became addicted while serving in Vietnam! Drugs were so accessible and so cheap!

On the convoy to Pr'Line, Randy and I rode in the back of a deuce-and-a-half and were able to see the beautiful city of Dalat. There were pictur-

esque homes with manicured lawns, and the "step" gardens on the outskirts of town were impressive, indeed. One would not know one was in a war zone. People went about their lives as if we were not there. Yes, there was evidence that a war had been there by the bombed-out shell of a church and several other buildings, but for the most part the town of Dalat was thriving.

As our convoy proceeded, however, the terrain became more ominous. We began to enter into the dense vegetation growth and experience the vile odor emitting from some of the small villages through which we traveled. The smell could take one's breath away. It finally dawned on me that the evening news that I had seen back home began to look like my present surroundings. I prayed that the soldiers on this convoy were better trained in combat than I. This was the first time in Vietnam that I feared for my life.

Upon arrival on Pr'Line, we got to the essentials before the sun would set in a couple of hours. Sergeant Parten showed Mike and me to our hooch. We each had a small room in the six-room dusty and bug-ridden building. Next, we were assigned to a bunker. These were fortified holes cut into the berm. Layers of corrugated metal, railroad ties and sandbags lined the sides and top of the bunkers. Large rats had free roam on Pr'Line, and cobras and three steppers were among us. We were told that if bitten by a three stepper, one had three steps before death. True or not, we believed it to be true. I encountered one of each of these snakes during my tour of duty. The cobra made sphincter muscles slam shut! I did the "Moonwalk" before the dance step had a name. After peeking inside my bunker, bunker number six, I swore an oath that I would never set foot in it!

Next our Sergeant took us to the mess hall. I'm sure I ate there through the year, yet I have only one memory of being in this place. I remembered the cook breaking eggs into a bowl, one at a time, trying unsuccessfully to find an egg that wasn't bad. Occasionally we had C-rations. I think these were made available when we were off the hill. The military issued P-38 can opener, needed for opening the C-rations, was a useful tool. I carry my P-38 on my key chain to this day! Amazingly, as our group has reunited, none of us can remember eating in the mess hall. Since what goes up must come down and typically what goes in must come out, we were next shown the

Menz's bunker, number six

three-hole toilet and cautioned with further instructions. Alongside the toilet, a six-inch diameter medal tube rose from the ground with a small privacy fence, labeled with this vital information – 4U2P. Other necessary introductions, such as "Tropo" would be necessary in the coming days.

That evening all of Tropo, except for the three men working the communication vans, had a "newbie celebration" for Mike and me. Everyone seemed to be older. One was twenty-six, five years older than I, yet in reality, everyone else just appeared older. Fatigues were faded, tattered and torn, faces were tinted, if not tainted by the environment. Attention to creased trousers, clean boots and military rank were all unimportant. The contrast to our initial differences proved irrelevant. These men were to become my family.

How do you spell relief?

On special occasions, such as this night, the men of Tropo would open a tin canister of Ritz crackers. This was a common item found in "care packages" sent from home and cherished on the hill. I remember when Tex (we never called him Jim), our senior member of Tropo, accidentally dropped a Ritz cracker on the concrete floor and the dust splashed from the impact, as if the cracker had fallen on flour. Tex immediately picked up the cracker, took a deep breath and blew off the dust. Into his mouth it went as he savored the morsel. *My soul*, I remember thinking, *this guy has been here for a while*! It wasn't long, however, until I acclimated and caught up with this veteran and other collective practices.

> **Ottens***: We loved getting care packages. My mom would send Chef Boyardee pizzas. We would cook them in an electric skillet and then everyone enjoyed the pizzas.*

We had some exposure to the communication vans while training at Fort Monmouth, but nothing like the rapid learning curve we experienced on the hill. Tropo was short for "tropospheric scatter tactical microwave communication." To oversimplify, we ricocheted microwave signals, coded with communication, off the troposphere to the intended receiver. This allowed for a greater distance than simple "line of sight" communication. Secret and highly classified communications passed through our equipment. Because of this, all of us in Tropo had top secret security clearances. Before the microwave was used for cooking, it was used for communication. More information to the previous sentence will be offered in chapter three. Yes, we did find a way to cook with our equipment.

The 362nd Signal Company (Tropo), was a part of the 73rd Signal Battalion, 21st Signal Group, 1st Signal Brigade. The 362nd was not the only company on Pr'Line. The other primary Signal Company was the 556 (mountain men). The motto of Tropo was "keep the shooters talking."

Even though most of us on Pr'Line have some amazing stories to share, and I will share a few, our primary job was to facilitate communication in its various forms, including teletype. This was the purpose of Pr'Line.

On the hill also was a company of soldiers from the Army of the Republic of Vietnam (ARVN) and most importantly, the 194th and the 61st M.P. Companies. Pr'Line was the headquarters for the 61st. They offered the protection for the hill and the many convoy missions to pick up supplies, mail and water. Even though mixing of the M.P.'s and Tropo was minimal, honored respect was mutual.

2

INTERFACING WITH
THE NATIVES

~IN BETWEEN~

Life is lived
in Between.
Between air sucked dust
and rain splattered mud.
Between peak experiences
and personal valleys.
Between the beauty of the forest
and the horror of the trees. (RLM)

* * * *

A CULTURAL PRACTICE THAT is not celebrated in the West is the lunar New Year or Tet Nguyen Dan, or merely Tet. Most of us who are veterans have a negative response to Tet, remembering the Tet offensive of 1968. This Tet offensive is believed to be the seismic shift that started the erosion of support for the war.

Yet for the Vietnamese, Tet is the most important annual festival that is both a public holiday and a major religious event. The day before Tet involves temple sacrifices and spiritual invitations for deceased ancestors to join in the festivities. Days after the New Year (usually in late January or early February) are filled with celebrations hailing the advent of spring.

This veteran remembers driving past a Tet parade while on a convoy to Cam Ranh Bay and having the wits scared from me. The village was filled with color and merriment, and I vicariously shared in the excitement as I drove by. What I wasn't expecting was the many packets of fire-crackers that burst as I drove by, an unwelcomed rush.

Relating with the Vietnamese, apart from the momasans, was very restricted. We would sometimes negotiate (argue) over prices in some of the open-air market places in Dalat. These were encounters born more from curiosity than that of need. The PX at the larger bases and the Pacix catalog offered everything one could imagine, if one was in a buying mood.

There were ARVNs stationed on Pr'Line, as has been previously mentioned, yet we seldom mingled. These soldiers

Tet parade in nearby village

were allowed to enter the Noncommissioned Officers (NCO) club, but they were restricted to the back when we were showing a movie or having entertainment from a musical group – usually from the Philippines. The ARVNs on Pr'Line were representative of the Vietnamese cultures of the Central Highlands. That is, they were composed of the Viet people and the Montagnard people. The Montagnard's (which means "people of the mountain") were the indigenous people of the Central Highlands. Their dwellings of bamboo and thatch were located on steep mountain slopes all around Pr'Line. Before forced into military uniforms, they were typically un-encumbered with clothing. The Montagnard soldiers were heavily recruited by South Vietnam because of their antipathy to the strong centralized state offered by North Vietnam.

There were many times that we connected with children in nearby Phat Chi. They would run to the edge of the road and wave, sometimes yelling, "GI number one!" These kids had learned early on that the GIs would likely

The author with some children in Phat Chi

have candy and treats to share. The communications beyond smiles and friendly gestures, however, were limited.

Ottens: *When our water well for Pr'Line was poisoned or broken down, we needed to go off the hill to get water every two or three days. I usually went to get the water and became known as "Water-boy." Some of the roads in our area were more dangerous than others. I chose to drive through the small villages and I became identified with the children. I slowed down through these villages, and tossed items from our sundry packs (candy, gum, paper, pens, shoelaces, cigarettes) to the children and villagers. My truck was easy to identify as I had an office chair in the machine gun mount to make it easier for me to observe when the tanks were full of water. The villagers were excited to see my truck coming and would come running. For the most part, I never had problems going through the villages.*

So, back to the momasan. In Vietnam, and much of Asia, this is the term given to a mother or a woman in a position of authority. We also inferred that "popasan" referred to a man of similar status. Even though we understood this meaning, to us, momasan primarily meant "maid."

Singleterry: *I have good memories of the momasans. Ting was my momasan, and her sister, Sun, later helped, though she didn't stay long. I can't remember the names of the others. They usually cooked their lunch on a hot plate on the floor of our hooch. At one point, they quit eating hot lunches for several days. When we ask why, they said the hot plate stopped working. Someone had a good idea to join the broken heating coil with a bolt and nut and it worked like a charm.*

When monsoon season came and it was cold at night, Ken reminded me that I received the nickname "Snow White" because I often wore my long johns. Later someone mentioned that I could get a lined rain jacket by supplying a blanket and poncho. A friend magically produced the required supplies and Ting took one measurement across my outstretched arms and one from my collar to my waist. In a couple of days, I had a warm, lined rain jacket with a hood that fit perfectly. That was the best $10.00 I ever spent.

The momasans were vetted, and in our case paid for, by the military. Most of our momasans were from the nearby

A typical "laundromat"

village of Phat Chi. Their clothing consisted of baggy-legged slacks, usually black and fabric thin. All wore "conical" hats. Their ages ranged from teenagers to older women. They all seemed attentive to neatness and cleanliness. However, the GIs noticed two exceptions to this. It was often, if not always, that momasans came to work with a strong smell of garlic. The other thing that caught us by surprise was that the elderly momasans had purple teeth. We were told that this resulted from chewing betel nut, the fruit of an areca tree. This nut was a mild stimulant like tobacco. Beyond the effects of a buzz drug, the Vietnamese people harbored long held ritual exercises to darken teeth as a part of their traditional practices and beliefs.

For the Tropo portion of Pr'Line, we had a half dozen momasans or so, that cleaned our hooches, laundered our clothes and made up our beds. I can still see their faces and remember some of their names. The one I would like to say more about is my momasan, Ven. I'm not sure how Ven spelled her name. It might have been spelled Venh, Vhen, Vin, Vinh or a number of other ways. There is a large city in the northern part of Vietnam by the name of the Vinh. Perhaps this is how Ven spelled her name. Yet, here in, I will refer to my momasan as Ven.

Ven was working on Pr'Line when I arrived in early September, 1970, and she remained when I left in late August of 1971. I was to learn that Ven was twenty-five years old when I arrived as a twenty-one-year-old. Ven had three children and was pregnant with number four. She had this baby boy sometime during my tour, and my memory is that she did not lose a single day of work from giving birth. I cherish several pictures of Ven, her three sons, one daughter, and her husband.

Momasan Ven and her beautiful family

Every time I asked Ven what her husband did, she would say, "he finny army." In fact, many of our expressions of communication were a bastardization of French, English and military slang. The French held a significant presence in South Vietnam before the Americans did. Consequently, they left much of their language and many customs behind. The French called the people of the mountain, Montagnard, and it stuck. The GIs perverted this by referring to the natives as "mountain yards." If someone was considered pretty, momasan would say "*beaucoup dep*," (*beaucoup* was French and *dep* was Vietnamese), i.e., "much pretty."

Another phrase was "*hieu biet*" for "understand." The GI would often say "bic" for *biet*. As in, "do you bic it?" There were countless phrases uttered by the Vietnamese thinking they were speaking English and the GIs thinking they were speaking Vietnamese. Some phrases were easily picked up on such as number one for good and number ten for bad. How about *dinky-dau or choi-oi*. Then there was the ever present, "No sweat."

Buddhism was by far the most common religion in Vietnam, yet most families in Phat Chi, if they were religious, were Roman Catholic. In addition to the orphanage that was operated by catholic priests, there was an influential Catholic church in town.

> **Brogan***: I actually went to mass at this church once – only once. Everyone had to leave their weapons in the foyer. I noticed as I positioned my M-16 on the floor, that there were also AK-47s (weapons of the North) positioned nearby. I resolved to never return.*

Most of the people in the Central Highlands were naturally suspicious. They were typically uncomfortable with having their pictures taken. The concern was that their pictures, frozen in time, could somehow capture their soul. For similar reasons, they resisted recording devices. After a few months, Ven relaxed these strict views. I not only have numerous pictures of Ven and her family, I was privileged to interview her on a cassette recording. By the end of the one-hour tape, several other momasans joined in conversation and in singing a Vietnamese song. Since the reuniting of the men of the

362nd, I have been able to share this recording with many of my Tropo brothers.

Ven not only had an engaging personality, she had a laugh that was contagious. I treasure her laughter every time I replay the cassette tape. In addition, her wit and sense of humor was unique and classically Ven. Whenever she saw me, she would say, "Bob, what you do?" It meant "how are you doing?" and she knew the difference, but delighted in grammatical mischief. Another of her favorite sayings was: "You want me to think about that?" This was spoken with her accent when she didn't understand something. And this was followed by her amusement and her laughter.

One of my most memorable times with Ven was when she invited half a dozen of us from the hill to her home for a Sunday dinner. Her entire family was there, including her parents. By this time, Ven and her husband had just finished the building of their new home. As photos have helped my memory, the house was about fifteen feet by twenty feet. The siding was wooden plank boards, the floor was concrete and the roof was tin. This home was upscale as most dwellings in Phat Chi had dirt floors and thatched roofs.

Most of us gathered outside the front of her home as there wasn't room for all of us to be inside at the same time. Ven had a gas stove supporting a large metal pot. She was proud to show us the two or three chickens being boiled within.

This vet was born and raised in rural Missouri, and remembered us butchering chickens for Sunday dinner. The process, after beheading the bird, was to remove the internals. Then we scalded it to make the plucking of the feathers easier. Lastly, the singeing of the tiny hair that covered the body was a very important step.

When I looked into Ven's pot, I learned that the removal of the small hair from the chicken was of no concern. Ven was so happy to serve us guys with a great meal, and we all embraced her generosity with genuine hunger. "When in Phat Chi, do as the Phat Chi!"

Another norm that Asian people enjoy that many from the West do not, is the use of fish oil. Nuoc Mam, as it is called in native tongue, is a fermented sauce made from fish or krill and has been a seasoning staple in Asia for millennia. There are few foods that can trigger a gag reflex for the western palate more than this sauce. The Vietnamese people season most of their food with this oil, and Ven abundantly embraced this custom. Even Kool Aid was spiked with Nuoc Mam. This smell added to the fragrance of Vietnam.

Our gathering was a full afternoon event. The chicken, the rice, the Kool Aid and the hospitality were remarkable! At Tropo's first reunion, we fondly remembered this day.

Even though this was, perhaps, my most meaningful meal in Vietnam, it was certainly not the most technologically advanced. Remember in chapter two, I said that before microwaves were used for cooking, they were used for communication. This is true in a general sense, but we specifically invalidated this notion on Pr'Line. Several of us proved time and time again that we could cook food with our equipment. Our large thirty-foot parabolic dishes are what we used to bounce the tropospheric scatter microwave signal off the troposphere to its intended receiver.

We were told that should we ever get on the transmitting side of these dish antennas, it would "Fry" us. Further, we were informed that if any one got within a certain peripheral angle from the dish, it would render that one sterile and impotent. This information was of greater concern than being "Fried."

I'm not sure who the first one was to test the frying idea, but someone did. If the microwave could cook a person, someone reasoned, it should be able to cook food.

Here's how it worked. The dishes were elevated about ten feet from the ground, and a ladder (of sorts) on the back side of the antenna spanned from the ground to a horizontal platform in the middle of the dish. Once on the platform, one could tie the food onto a rope and throw the rope over the top side of the dish – about fifteen feet up. Then the "food on a rope" could be lowered to the transmitter, or focal point of the dish. The signal was indeed intense. The food was overcooked or burned, more often than not. We cooked chickens, a dear shoulder and canned goods. Typically, however, these efforts were individual and mostly experimental.

The one thing I cooked from one of our parabolic dishes was a can of spam. As I lowered the spam to the transmitter's center, the energy pushed the rope and spam out several inches. *Wow*, I thought, *this really could fry us*. I held the spam in place for only a few seconds, and it was cooked. I had to wait a while before I could touch the can and share my meal. Yes, all the while, I took all the necessary precautions to avoid impotence!

By far, our meal with Ven, was for me, the most meaningful. Cooking with our equipment was "cutting edge" challenging. Albeit, the most memorable meal was, well, unforgettable. Mike, Marc and Jerry tell the story.

Brogan: *By good fortune, Rosie, my fiancé, kept all the letters I wrote to her throughout the year. Because of this, I was able to reconstruct a particularly unusual event. Tet New Year fell on January 26, 1971. On January 22, Bob Menz, Jerry Sharp, Marc Bourque and myself were invited to a Vietnamese soldier's house in commemoration of the Tet holiday.*

In spite of the fact that we spoke no Vietnamese and our hosts spoke no English, our festive evening included a wonderful meal with the main ingredient being, what we first believed to be pork. The color implied pork, the taste suggested pork, however, the fat was unusually tough. We also had tasty soup with slivers of black meat mixed with the yummy noodles. The soup was explainable, even before we clarified the soups ingredients. In another hooch, at a previous time, we had the same kind of soup. The noodles were ramen, the slivers of meat were rat. All was good. We did not grow tails or lose fingernails.

The "pork" was a little more challenging to nail down. A direct question revealed that the meat was dog. Bob and I remembered the family's pet dog being present up until the day of that fine dinner, and the dog was to never be seen again. This was not just a dog; it was their dog. One can only assume the family pet had become our gourmet main course. The night concluded with cake and candy.

The next four days following that dinner was a story in itself. Bob and I apparently suffered from food poisoning and we were quite ill. However, over the years, I came to appreciate the generosity of our host. They gave their best with what little they had, as they attempted to please us during their revered Tet holiday.

Sharp: *I remember this meal. I had only been on the mountain a short time and felt honored to have been invited to go to this dinner with Mike, Marc and Bob. The ARVN soldier's home was small and built in a row with other ARVN homes right next to it. The home was clean with a bamboo mat placed on the floor. We were brought in and seated on the mat.*

The four of us and the ARVN were all who were eating. The soldier's wife was in the doorway just outside the house with a large wok being heated by homemade charcoal. She put oil of some kind into the wok and added pieces of meat. The meat was cut into triangles and looked peculiar to me. It was a light-colored meat, with a layer of fat between the meat and also on top of it. She fried this in hot oil and then added noodles. This was put into small bowls and passed to us. I remember that I ate the noodles, but not the meat. The ARVN asked, "You no like the meat?" I said something, and the subject changed. Then Mike asked what the meat was. The ARVN said, "bark, bark." Yep, it was confirmed that the meat was dog. I felt good that I had passed on the meat.

Next the wife took what looked like rice paper and placed water on it. Vegetables and the dark colored meat were then added and fried in the wok. They were like egg rolls and were served alongside soup made with the same meat. I ate both of these and had a second eggroll. They were actually very good. Then, of course, Mike asked what this meat was. The soldier gestured and answered, "squeak, squeak. The mystery was solved; it was rat! I remember returning to our hooch and laughing about dining on rat and dog. I recall that Mike and Bob got sick for a couple of days after the meal. Fortunately, I did not.

Bourque: *This meal occurred at a Vietnamese officer's house. I was there the day before and was introduced to the dog. I grew up with dogs as pets and remember this mixed breed dog being very friendly and probably only two or three months old. The dog was noticeably missing the day of our gathering. After the meal, Mike asked the Vietnamese officer what the meat was that was served with the noodles. When he responded, "bow-wow, bow-wow," it became clear to all of us!*

The only thing I can add here is to say that this was the best rat and the best dog I've ever had! Furthermore, this was the last rat and the last dog I've ever had! After this, I was much less worried about the unsinged hair on Ven's chickens. Albeit, one should not consider these different dishes outside the context of cultural norms.

Thomas: *I spent many nights visiting with the ARVN's, in their homes. We would usually have a snack (no meat) and a shot or two of Sake or rice wine. Usually, Ott and Snow-white joined in these visits. I remember conversations with one young officer in particular. He was twenty something and very well educated. He spoke English and French and I could understand French fairly well. This allowed for stimulating conversations about the war and philosophical speculations as to how it might end. This ARVN officer was a very interesting person and we shared many similar views. Unfortunately, we were told by the "brass" that we could no longer go down to the ARVN location and so our visits ended and our lives moved on.*

Ven was not only good at cooking and entertaining, she appeared to be more culturally informed than other momasans on the hill. She seemed to have an historical understanding of the war and a realistic discernment of what lay ahead. I have been troubled through the years as I recount Ven's haunting concern: "I think that maybe when Americans go home, the North will kill us in Phat Chi." This was a real concern, because many in this small village were known to support the American initiative in various ways. They were also "in the know" when it came to VC activity. They seemed to have their "ears to the rail" and would warn us of dangers and travel concerns. When Ken returned to Pr'Line in 1994, he learned that the Vietnamese military had assumed possession of the mountain and guarded it intently. Our concern of Ven's fears seem confirmed.

> **Ottens:** *In 1994 I was able to return to Pr'Line Mountain. At that time, my family and I were missionaries in the Philippines, and I was developing a maintenance program for the Philippine Missionary Institute that was part of Action International Ministries. Along with two other Action missionaries, Larry Russ and Glenn Johnson, I went back to Vietnam. Glenn and his family had been missionaries in Dalat during the war. Toward the end of the war, Glenn sent his family home, and later he was on the last civilian flight out of Vietnam.*
>
> *The roads to Pr'Line were still very familiar to me, but when I arrived, soldiers said I was not allowed inside the gate. After much discussion, I was allowed inside the gate with instructions to not take any pictures. They had some questions about the two big holes by the entrance. I remembered that this was where we had our flags and told them that these were holes left when our flag poles were removed. They appreciated getting this concern solved. As gestures of friendship were offered, protocol was relaxed. By the end of my visit, I could take as many pictures as I wanted. I was able to sit on the ground where my hooch once stood, my home in the clouds. I also was able to put my foot up on the stone fireplace we had built. Noticing that most of the structures were gone I asked about*

Nearby farmer using water buffalo to plow. Notice the "stair-stepped" children

the momasans in Phat Chi. I was informed that they were gone too. The Vietnamese soldiers reported that they had all died mysteriously... stepped on a mine or drowned in the ocean. These were mountain people. I can't believe they would be going to the ocean. This is so sad.

As conversations continued, I was able to have tea with the commanding officer at the site. Through an interpreter, we talked about our families. When I stood up to leave, he pointed to a picture of his children and said, "The war was not good, and we need to make things better for our kids."

3

SACRIFICES AND LONELINESS

~MISGUIDED~

War's selfish desires
Did not consider
Could only deliver
Cruel suffering and pain.

War's insatiable greed
Could not account
For the amount
Of anguish its actions would create.

War's distortions of purpose
And the assumption of truth
Were the ultimate proof
That hurt was justified.

War's misguided ideology
Projected a point of view
Focused and displayed on you, and in you,
That this was the only paradigm. (RLM)

* * * *

FIRST OF ALL, WHEN it comes to sacrifices, the loved ones of those deployed made great sacrifices and suffered monumental losses. This veteran did not have children at that time, but I was married. Years later, the relationship ended in divorce. During this time frame, the pained separation was due only to the war. Many of the service men had wives and children. In addition, mothers and fathers of these GIs suffered many sleepless nights with recurring nightmares and "daymares." My mother informed me during this time that if I considered going to Canada, she and my father would make it happen. My parents understood that this was no real option for me.

I remember looking out of the plane's window in St. Louis when I was preparing to depart for Vietnam, and on the tarmac was my wife and my mother and my father standing so alone – so alone. "Will I ever see them again?" I wondered.

Most everyone who served in Vietnam made sacrifices. It is generally understood that over 58,000 made the ultimate sacrifice. Of the approximately 3.4 million that were deployed to Southeast Asia, over 153,000 thousand were wounded (with nearly that many more that were wounded and not hospitalized). Nearly 11,000 died (in theater) from causes not directly related to the war. This of course is dwarfed by health issues that have presented since 1975. Illnesses such as Agent Orange exposure, Hepatitis C, Post Traumatic Stress Disorder (PTSD) and numerous other illnesses and maladies have resulted in mounting sacrifices that are difficult to measure.

Singleterry: *Typically those of us in Tropo did not have to pull guard duty. However, on a couple of occasions, I did have to stand lonesome guard from my bunker. I took my binoculars with me to pass the time, but I found looking at the grass waiving in the wind mesmerizing, like trying to drive in a snowstorm with snow blowing every which way. I tried to imagine I could see someone sneaking through the grass trying to figure out how they could get close enough to turn the clay-mores around facing our bunkers, as we had found them on several occasions. It would have been easier to see what was going on beyond the berm lights if the vegetation had been removed to the tree line. It didn't occur to me to ask someone about solving this problem, and apparently it didn't occur to those who could offer the fix, to do so.*

One night, when the siren beckoned us to our bunkers, the rapid fire of the M-16 to my left quickly ended the hearing in my left ear. After the disorientation and vomiting stopped, I still could not hear in my left ear. Or more accurately, all I could hear was the loud ringing. I was to later receive ten percent disability for hearing loss and ten percent disability for tinnitus. It is impossible to hear what someone is saying to me when my good ear is on the phone. Also, many have wondered why I swing around my right ear when someone tries to whisper in my left ear.

After I experienced hip pain in my late forties, I was

later diagnosed with osteoporosis when I was fifty years old. This is a disease that elderly women get, right? Well, ten years later my endocrinologist determined to get to the bottom of why a fifty-year-old man would develop osteoporosis. Several months went by before my doctor learned that I had Monoclonal Gammopathy of unknown significance (MGUS). This later became MGUS multiple myeloma (bone marrow cancer). Within months, the office of veteran's affairs awarded me an additional sixty percent disability for the exposure to Agent Orange that resulted from serving in Vietnam. My name isn't on the Vietnam Memorial in D.C. (and I'm glad it isn't and do not believe it should be), yet I will likely die as a result of my exposure to Agent Orange while serving in Vietnam.

Bridge over troubled waters between Pr'Line and Cam Ranh

4

MOMENTS OF FEAR

~VC~

Deep fried – tie dyed
Strings abide – lie
Sigh – die
Why (RLM)

* * * *

I WAS ON PR'LINE (the hill) for about two weeks when I was awakened in the middle of the night with the rapid-fire sound of M-16s, the concussive sounds of a .50-caliber, and the screaming shrill of our alert siren. The siren was like the warning signal that alerts residents of an approaching tornado. In our case, it signaled the concern of approaching enemy. I had already developed a practice of having my clothes, boots, helmet and weapon in place to grab and run. Grab and run I did. Within seconds, I was running toward my bunker. When I reached bunker number six, I dove into it like it was a swimming pool. So much for my oath!

This was the first of many nights that I became intimate with my bunker. Most of these "Alerts" were false alarms.

It could have been that someone appeared over the berm and then disappeared. Animals were sometimes mistaken for Viet Cong (VC) and perhaps sometimes it was the over imagination of anxious guards. During these times we would plant rounds of lead into the jungle, lob a few mortars beyond the tree line, wait for an hour or so and then go back to bed (usually not back to sleep). There were a few times, however, that we were compelled to continue carving back the jungle with boxes of ammunition. Flares would illuminate the darkness of the night, and only in our fears and imagination did we envision the North Vietnamese army (NVA), or the VC (also called "Charley") climbing our hill.

In fact, Pr'Line was relatively secure as an isolated compound. We were told that the VC would bounce their small radio signals off our powerful antennas and increase their range. For this reason, it was advantageous to the VC and the NVA for the Pr'Line site to exist. We attained a bit of security from this notion, but only a bit.

Where we were the most vulnerable was when we left the perimeter of the hill. Particularly were our convoys in harm's way. A dear Tropo friend, Zeke, had his leg broken when his jeep went off the road after the convoy was hit with a rocket. Another, David, spent ten months in hospitals after tripping a land mine (Zeke has since passed and David joins our monthly zoom). Most common was sniper fire from unknown locations in the dense jungle or crowded hamlets. There was yet another time that our convoy was ambushed. It was learned very quickly, that the convoy was attacked by the very ARVN's that were supposed to be guarding Pr'Line mountain.

It was difficult to know who was going to turn against

An explosion from mortars lobbed into the tree line by the MPs

you. Our momasans were vetted by the military and the constant interfacing with them offered levels of confidence that built our trust. Albeit, a Vietnamese woman who was hired to work in our NCO club, was revealed to be VC! This soldier never went alone to the Vietnamese barber on the hill. All this uncertainty regarding who was safe, added to our fear. Were the ones that tended to be friendly truly our friends? On this subject, there was an absence of light. That is, the lack of clarity with this distinction wasn't always present. Preeminent understanding was in the clouds.

I had not been in country long enough for my fatigues to fade when our return convoy was detained past the deadline to return to Pr'Line. All road traffic had to be off the road and in the terminal destination by 1800 hours. For reasons long forgotten, we missed this return window from Dalat. Perhaps we were delayed because someone got lost on their mission. More likely someone's vehicle broke down and others had to rescue them and the broken-down truck. Here in, the reason doesn't matter. The point of this story will be clear.

Checkpoint x-ray, at the edge of town, was the spot where we would split up and accomplish our individual assignments. We would reassemble at a prearranged time at this same checkpoint. X-ray was also where Ann's House was. Ann's House was a bar and simple food restaurant. There were several cute girls on the premises, yet probably not on the payroll. These young ladies were not hookers, they just added atmosphere. Hookers were down the street at Madam Thais.

Well, whoever was in charge of the convoy, arranged for us to stay over in the hotel rooms above Ann's House. This was the first time I was to stay overnight at a location other than a military compound. This was to happen two other times, on separate occasions in Saigon, yet the lessons learned on this night were not forgotten.

We decided to have a beer in the bar section before we retired to our rooms upstairs. We may have had another beer, because there was no TV, radio or books (in English) to pass our time.

At some point we were shown to our sleeping rooms. These were small quarters with a simple bunkbed for one person. This newbie was a bit concerned about this whole situation and decided to not disrobe or remove my M-16 from my side. I locked the door, had my hand on the pistol grip and ensured that it was "locked and loaded."

After a couple of hours, I was awakened by a Vietnamese woman who asked if she could join me.

"Get out!" I shouted. She saw my M-16 and indeed rushed out. *How did she get in?* I wondered. *Stupid question*, I concluded. I can actually remember and relive that fearful moment. Even now my heart is pounding as I reminisce. I resolved to not fall asleep again that night and in other similar situations, never allow myself to sleep.

As it turned out, one of the guys did let her, or someone, sleep with him. For privacy reasons, I will call him Boots, because we had no one on the hill that we called Boots. Boots, unlike many of us on the hill, was not married. Even so, his actions were irresponsible and wrong on so many levels. The tragic outcome of this was that Boots contracted a serious STD and struggled for a cure for months.

> **Singleterry**: *I usually avoided the trip to Dalat unless I needed something from the PX, and as a general rule, preferred the relative safety of the hill to risking a trip on the road. I reluctantly did have to make a trip to Dalat for a promotion board. During this time, it was suggested that I get a haircut while there. The haircut was an experience I had not expected. The haircut went well with a lot of unnecessary snipping of the air in between cuts. Then came the ear cleaning, which apparently came with the haircut. I forgot who was urging me to go along with this because they thought it was a good deal. I thought the "barber" was going to poke my brain out as deep as he was going. He smiled and showed me how much wax he scooped out. I vowed to never let that happen again, and I didn't.*

*While preparing to return to the hill, I was asked
to move a jeep out of our way. I jumped in the
jeep and asked, "where's the key?" I felt like I
was the only one in Nam who didn't know that
military vehicles didn't have ignition keys. The
starter is located under one of the pedals. To this
day, I can't remember which one.*

Rarely were we totally free from fear. On Christmas Eve
1970, my friend John and I planned a trip to Don Bosco, a
Catholic orphanage a couple of kilometers away in the village
of Phat Chi. Many of us had visited these children before
and our presence was welcomed by the children and the
priests. Most of the kids were fathered by U. S. soldiers and
consequently had a stigma instead of a home. On this day,
we planned to bring a dozen or so back to Pr'Line and feed
them a Christmas dinner. As we attempted to drive out of the
Pr'Line perimeter, the gate guard told us that we could not
leave the hill without a weapon. "There is a truce, we don't
need a weapon," I replied! I had been "in country" for four
months and had no reason to be that naive. The fact that we
had a "ceasefire" did not mean that fire would cease! John
was driving the deuce-and-a-half and I was riding "shotgun."

"Here, take this." The guard presented me an M-79
grenade launcher. We were about 500 meters out of the
gate where we had to turn left or right. While waiting to
turn right and head for Phat Chi, a bus zoomed by filled
with Vietnamese, animals, crates, luggage and a sniper.
John and I dove to the floor board of the truck as bullets
flew by. The whole experience lasted three or four seconds,
yet I condensed in that time what felt like three or four

The Don Bosco Catholic Orphanage

hours of emotional bubbles popping within. I could have turned my M-79 toward the bus and removed the threat. I did not. I chose not. I needed not. That threat was going around the bend. Of all the decisions I made over there, this may have been the most important. I have never had to live with - whatever comes with, taking another's life.

It certainly was naïve of me to think that I needed no weapon while leaving the hill on Christmas Eve. Here is another story of equal absurdity. Shortly after arriving on Pr'Line, I was issued an M-79 grenade launcher along with the standard M-16. We also had access to other weapons including the M-60 machine gun. After being in country several months, I was able to purchase a Colt .45 pistol from a private party. The details of the purchase have been lost to time. At any rate, it was not issued to me by the Army. When on R&R in Hawaii, a Tropo brother,

Dan, volunteered to pick up the mail while I was gone. In addition, Dan asked if he could borrow my .45 while I was gone. I saw no problem with his request and loaned him the pistol. Upon my return from R&R, I learned that there were indeed reasons for concern. A matter substantial enough to get me called into our Captain's office.

The week that I was away, one of our convoys experienced a significant ambush. For some reason, Dan chose to take my colt and leave his M-16 behind. When the convoy was hit, Dan jumped into a deep roadside ditch and fired the pistol that was reached above his head. The nine or so rounds that were in the clip were all Dan had and they were gone in seconds. Dan said later, "I didn't even have a club to fight with." Well, His absence of shooting back was noticed. The next day, Dan was called to the Captain's office.

"Why didn't you have your M-16 with you?" asked the officer.

Dan responded, "It was definitely a mistake, I just felt like it was going to be an easy trip and I wouldn't need it."

"Where and how did you come about having a pistol that wasn't issued to you?"

"I borrowed it from Menz."

And so, this is why I was summoned to the Captain's office. Suffice it to say, my pistol was taken away. Fortunately, that was the only discipline I received.

Sharp: *When I awoke on the morning of this story, it was a clear day and warm. My friend Jerry Horn and I were planning to make a trip to Dalat that day. As I looked out over the vast view below our*

The author's arsenal

berm, it was as if I were looking down from a plane. The clouds were below us and the smell of fuel was in the air. We were both looking forward to getting off the mountain that day to break up the accumulated boredom that we felt. We hurried to get our gear and M-16s and headed toward the convoy site which was forming for the trip. Jerry and I got in the back of a deuce-and-a-half truck and the convoy was off. The road that we took ran down through some small towns and some very rough mountain passes, a distance I think was about fifteen to twenty kilometers. The view was pretty and quiet on the way down.

Once we passed a place called checkpoint "Charlie," about ten Kilometers, our escort fell off and waited for us to return from Dalat. When we arrived in Dalat, we went to Kraus compound and then broke up for what we each had to do. Some went to pick up mail, others were tasked to get certain supplies, yet others went on to the Airport and got fuel for our needs on the mountain. Jerry and I went to the Airport and helped with the fuel. Once this was done, we still had some time to kill before the convoy was to return to the mountain. Jerry and I and some others went to a small place nearby called Ann's House and had a few beers and waited for the convoy to form and leave for the mountain. Soon we got the call from the lieutenant to form up and head out. Jerry and I were in the back of the truck again with two other men and were happy to be making the trip back to the mountain. Before we left the bar, the ladies who worked there kept telling us not to go back that day but to stay the night. Of course, this was not going to happen, as most of us were married. However, it seemed funny that they would be saying this. Did they know something?

The convoy left and headed back up the winding road past checkpoint Charlie where our escort once again joined us. We had an APC with a .50-caliber gun to lead the way, followed by a couple deuce-and-a-half trunks. Then there was a ¾ ton truck that was driven by Bob Menz who had our mail as he was our volunteer mailman. Bob was also carrying several cases of soda pop which was going back to the mountain with us. Following were two more deuce-and-a-half trucks and a jeep with our Lieutenant in it. We had made our way up the mountain roads past a place called "Foxtrot," which was a switchback section with about five switchbacks to climb the mountain. Then our convoy passed some small towns and a place which proved to be the most dangerous location on the trip, a narrow roadcut we called "Claymore Alley." Once the APC was almost through the cut and the rest of the convoy was in the cut, there was a loud bang, and then small arms fire broke out all along the convoy from both sides. The trucks stopped and we all jumped out and took cover, where we could find it, and began returning fire. Jerry and I were behind a log which was up on a small rise of dirt, and I remember it had a lot of branches on it. Both Jerry and I saw a machine gun firing down on us, and we each shot a twenty-round magazine into it. We then fell to our backs and reloaded our M-16s. At this time branches and wood went flying up in every direction into the air, and dirt was being kicked up on the other side of where we lay. The log started coming apart above us. All that was going through my mind was that I was going to be killed in this land, so far from home, by people that I never knew. I was certain that I was going to die. I saw my life go before me. When I looked up again, the log with its branches was gone. We then scurried to another spot and continued returning fire.

Then there was a sound that I will not forget. It

was a slow boom, boom, boom. At first, I thought it was the VC or the NVA and fear ran through me as to what it was. It then occurred to me that it was our own .50-caliber on our APC, and just like that, it was over. We ran to the trucks and jumped in and tried to leave the pass. One of the 2-ton trucks and the ¾ ton would not start and the people jumped in our truck or on one of the other trucks and we left. I remember Bob grabbed the mail bag but had to leave the pop. We headed back up the mountain. This was my first time under fire, and I was shaken inside but never wanted anybody else to know. I think we all were, but we put on an air of, "just another day." I never talked about the attacks while on the mountain with anyone else, but it was always in my mind, and I never made as many trips off the hill after that day.

Upon returning to the mountain, there was a reaction force that went down to the ambush site and checked it out. They brought back the two trucks we had left. The reaction force said they found blood trails leaving the spot but no bodies. None of us was hit. The next day I was told that there were graveside services in the small towns by the ambush site, but I can't be sure. The trucks were repaired and we were all OK, but the pop in the ¾ ton was never found. I was very glad that Bob was able to save the mail. This was our lifeline to home, or the world, as we called it.

As I said before, this was my first combat, or coming under fire by the VC or NVA, and it had

Establishing a perimeter after a sniper attack near
Claymore Alley

*an effect on me. While I was in country after that,
I came under fire quite a few more times, but nothing ever stood out like this time.*

I am grateful to Jerry for recounting this story that many
in Tropo experienced and remember. For me, for some
unknown reason, this incident created a disturbance in my
personal "Space-Time Continuum." There is very little
about this day that I can remember.

Then there were fears that existed apart from the gestures
of war. Every night, before climbing into bed, I pulled the
sheets back to ensure that there was nothing slithering on
my bed – be it legless or otherwise. As I reflect on this
now, I am very grateful that I had a bed – every night!
That was not true for many U.S. soldiers. I had a hooch to
stay dry. Many GIs did not, at least not all of the time.

Further, some fear was generated by the unpredictable nature in which events unfolded.

> **Bourque***: Pr'Line Mountain had a communication link that connected Cam Ranh Bay with a communication van called Trac-90. From Cam Ranh, the signal continued to Nha Trang. When the VC blew up an ammunition dump in Cam Ranh Bay, it rendered the signal between these sites unfunctional. Daryl and I were the two Tropo guys charged with fixing this problem.*
>
> *After doing some troubleshooting in Cam Ranh, we determined that the remaining issue was the result of misalignment at the Nha Trang site. The next day, once the roads had been cleared for travel, Daryl and I headed toward Nha Trang in a deuce-and-a-half that was provided to us in Cam Ranh. We had traveled approximately half way, perhaps an hour, when the drive shaft came apart from the transmission. As we coasted to a stop, we noticed the sleeve/housing and the 4 nuts and bolts holding everything together were missing. There was no way we could repair the truck without these parts.*
>
> *After about a half hour of looking along the road for the missing part and hoping we would not be visited by VC, we were approached by a convoy headed toward Cam Ranh Bay. They wanted to help, but they did not have parts nor the means to tow us anywhere. They did assure us that they would send a wrecker.*

Approximately an hour after the convoy had left, we saw a Vietnamese boy walking toward us carrying something dangling from what looked like a short piece of wire. He asked, "GI you lose?" It was the sleeve that had come off of the transmission. We were ecstatic at what he had found and brought to us. We thanked him and gave him all of the soda we had brought for the trip.

Being technicians and not mechanics, we were ill equipped with proper tools to address the problem. Beyond that, we had to locate four bolts to hold the mechanism in place. However, problem solvers we became. We located one bolt that held the seat to the body that would work. One attaching the bumper that was the right size. A usable bolt on the windshield wipers seemed to work, as did one holding the gas can to the back of the truck. Well, to make a long story short, we got the truck put back together and headed back to Cam Ranh just before the roads closed at dark. Why the motor pool would send out a truck in that condition on Vietnamese roads made no sense. But much there made no sense. The whole ordeal accomplished unnecessary anxiety and little else. Daryl and I never made it to Nha Trang, but others fixed the Trac-90 problem.

An experience similar to the feelings that Marc expressed was felt by me the first time I went to Saigon while preparing for my departure on R&R. Leaving the hill a day early ensured I could process all necessary forms, in triplicate, given my allocated time frame. The flight from Dalat to Saigon was on the predictable C123. Upon arrival, I met another soldier who was also destined to Hawaii for his R&R. I do not remember his name but do remember his face as I took several pictures of him and our adventure.

We took a cab to a nearby hotel, in what felt like the center of the city, and booked a room for the night. We both felt fairly secure, but committed to take turns sleeping in the small sleeping room. I do not recall the details of guard duty but remembered my resolve to never sleep alone in a Vietnam hotel again. The night was uneventful and I awoke with the determined mission to get to Tan Son Nhat airport in plentitude.

When we went to the street to look for a cab, we saw only motorized cyclo taxis. These were motorcycles with a bench seat between two wheels in front and the driver steering from behind. The cyclo drivers were eager for our business and attempts at communication lead us to believe they could take us to the airport. I was on my cyclo and my fellow traveler was on his.

This whole journey to Saigon occurred without a weapon because we were expected to only be in places surrounded by military. Our concern began to peek when we traveled so far from where we began and the airport was not in sight. We found ourselves in dense traffic and surrounded by bicycles and motorcycles. Some of the cyclists had rifles slung over their shoulders. Could any of these armed men be snipers? We weaved in and out of congested traffic for about an hour and finally found ourselves at a port with many ships.

"This is not the airport! We need to be where the planes are!"

"Take a ship," he said.

Well, it was on! The driver wanted to be paid and we weren't paying. Fortunately, a Saigon policeman jumped in and asked what was going on. When we explained, the police called a taxi to take us to the Tan Son Nhat airport and we were on our way. I'm not sure if we miscommunicated or if we were the object of a cruel joke. At any rate, we paid only the taxi driver that took us to the airport and arrived unscathed and in sufficient time.

I am mindful of and offer honor to all of my many brothers and a few sisters who experienced great pain in mind, body and spirit. Many harbored fears that others could not fathom. Many Vietnam veterans have stated that their tour involved long bouts of haunting boredom with intermittent spurts of extreme terror.

5

ERAS OF BOREDOM

~AVOIDING ENNUI~

Like snowflakes
we are all unique.
As with snowflakes
cold facilitates survival. (RLM)

* * * *

D URING OUR TIMES OF boredom, we became fairly creative with attempts to entertain. First there was the army's efforts to minimize boredom. We had an NCO club, and the NCO had beer. Most of us in Tropo wrapped our stomachs around a couple of beers in a respectfully consistent manner. There may have been occasions when our livers were stimulated – but not often. In retrospect, we were responsible on many levels.

Pr'Line, like many military sites, had "druggies" and "juicers." Juicers were the ones who drank alcohol. Druggies wanted to alter their consciousness with substances not sold in the NCO club. At least not over the counter. We only had a couple of men in Tropo that over-experimented with drugs. This behavior was simply shunned.

Entertainment in Pr'Line's NCO club

Perhaps most of the guys in Tropo had at least "tried" marijuana – or pot. This was not the case for Marc, Mike or me. We didn't judge those who smoked pot, but we had no desire to even try it, and others in Tropo knew this.

On one evening, several were gathered in someone's room smoking pot. The attic access door was opened to allow for better ventilation. Either the large rat in the attic was clumsy or perhaps had inhaled too much smoke. At any rate, the rat fell on one of the guys. He grabbed the rat and through it to the floor. However, before the rat was fully released, it bit him. The unfortunate result was that the rat was able to scurry away. Without being able to test the rat for rabies, this poor GI had to endure a series of painful rabies shots for a lengthy amount of time.

On a lighter note, toward the end of my tour (and Mike's), several of our buddies combined pizzas from their care packages and made pizza for all. We did not know until just before we left the hill that the pizzas were sprinkled with pot. Neither Mike or me actually felt or noticed anything at that time. As for the others, they sure got a laugh when they told us how they had spiked our pizza!

Two other forms of entertainment offered at the club were movies and live musical entertainment. Recently, I again went through my military paraphernalia and found my authorization card permitting me to operate the 16-mm projector. I do not remember operating the movie projector many times, but I do remember that seldom was a movie shown that was worth watching.

The live music, however, was a different story. We had six to eight groups that came to the hill and performed at the club during my tour of duty. These were highly anticipated programs with greatly prepared musicians. These exciting evenings were usually followed by slow mornings.

During our boring times, some of us played cards, mostly bridge. This vet remembers playing bridge for four to six hours at a setting.

A far more rigorous activity than playing cards was engaging in clothes fights. Clothes fights involved pulling and tearing the fatigues off each other until one of the two had nothing left to tear. This practice went on for days until Sergeant Brown (who replaced Sergeant Parten) brought it to an abrupt end.

A similar activity occurred several times during the monsoon season. Why we thought that mud wrestling was fun escapes me now. Especially considering the fact that Ken had to truck our water in and showers were seldom an option. In fact, I remember brushing my teeth and rinsing with a soda in the absence of water.

Another activity that we all embraced were the Tropo barbecues. These were real barbecues, and not our "microwave" attempts at cooking! These were such meaningful communal occasions that we all had stories about them at our first reunion. Now to be clear, the most meaningful meal was at Ven's, and the most memorable meal was the rat/dog soup. Yet, the barbecues were occasions for bonding. The attempts to cook from our antennas were solitary and not community occasions. During the 1970/71 timeframe, we all pitched in and built a barbecue pit. It was huge! Later, one or two of our guys added a chimney to carry the smoke away from our Tropo communication vans.

As stated earlier, when Ken returned to Pr'Line in 1994, even though most of the buildings were gone, he noticed that the barbecue pit remained. The pictures he brought back revealed the pit to be no worse for wear.

Gathering around the recently built BBQ firepit

Ken played a central role in locating the steaks and other items we cooked (choosing to never barbecue a dog). I'm not sure how Ken was able to pull off such feats. Suffice it to say, he had connections. On one occasion, beef steaks arrived in a container with dry ice. After close inspection, it was determined that the steaks were spoiled.

"What the hell," someone said, "we are all spoiled." We cooked the meat, albeit a little longer than usual, and we ate. No one got sick.

There were also occasions where we spent time in a more reflective and meditative ways. My friend Tex captures this sentiment in the following story:

> **Thomas**: *I am impressed with a memory I have of sitting on top of our hooch one night and watching a huge group of thunderstorms light up the valley towards Saigon. We could see for forty or fifty miles and it was a tremendous display of God's power. We watched for a couple of hours and came to realize how insignificant we are on this earth.*

I remember that evening, or more likely, one similar to it. There were times, if so inclined, one could be in harmony with nature. Early mornings were usually quiet, and with intentionality, one could transcend the reality of war and be in synch with the universe. With the carpet of white clouds beneath the berm, there was for this vet a peaceful, haunting, mesmerizing experience. The experience could take one's breath away. Then again, under those clouds was a threat that could indeed take one's breath away – literally. To be sure, all of our brotherhood has shared special memories of being In the Clouds.

Most of the times that I witnessed the clouds, they seemed static. There were, however, a couple of time that the clouds moved like gentle waves on an otherwise calm lake. The movement seemed to generate even greater tranquility – bordering on the sacred. Now I wonder, did this quiet time of meditation constitute prayer? Can an outburst of joy be prayer? Does a smile need words to become prayer? Does a tear need verbal accompaniment to be prayer?

On these mornings, it was easy to be overwhelmed with beauty. The contrast of the white clouds below and the blue sky above. The spotty shades of emerald vegetation visible on other mountain tops. On one occasion, I wanted to go out and touch these clouds when I realized, these clouds had reached out and touched me.

This vet had ways of contrasting tranquil times with more eventful activities. The main way this veteran avoided

Post Office in Dalat where the author picked up mail

getting sedentary was to venture off the hill. Our convoys were potentially risky adventures, but never boring. My main responsibility, apart from my duties with the 362nd, as has been mentioned, was to pick up our mail. As Pr'-Line's mailman, I would pick up mail in Dalat a couple times per week.

Most of us had a generous portion of denial. I knew that people got shot, but I didn't think I would ever be one of them. I thank God I wasn't. I sometimes worried about my friends being hurt or killed, yet my own psychological defenses would not allow me to consider my own death – not really.

The denial of death is a universal force existing far beyond war. Brought face to face with death, we are capable of blocking it, denying it, or fantasizing it away. We have even successfully substituted words for death. That is, she has passed, or he has expired. The person is not dying, he or she is terminal.

We know that death occurs on our highways, yet, we do not entertain the notion that we may be one of the dead when we travel. This, of course, is also true with other accidents and illnesses. When the "deceased" are not known, the information is not personal. If we are in various ways emotionally involved with someone who dies, it is an interpersonal loss and, here, we grieve. However, when we wrestle with our own being or not being, forces of denial are typically at work within us.

Our culture gives attention to aggressive, vigorous individuals filled with boundless energy. It is understandable that death, the direct opposite of such vital life is denied. Some try to defy death; most people deny it. We cognitively understand that people die, yet, most of us ignore considering ourselves among the "fatalities."

Wanderlust, my passion, my boundless energy and my vigor has always been a part of my life. This was present in Vietnam while traveling in convoys! My friend, Ken Ottens, apparently had a similar venturous spirit. Ken volunteered to be our water-boy. He would travel to a reservoir or river and bring back large tanks of water for us to use on the hill. Most frequently, Ken would fill his tanks from the reservoir in Don Doung, about ten or fifteen kilometers from the hill. I accompanied Ken on many of these trips. Beyond these convoys, many of us would travel to Dalat, Cam Ranh, Nha Trang and other places to get supplies and equipment for Tropo.

Dalat was, and I understand still is, one of the most beautiful cities in Vietnam. The French influenced architecture and culture was remarkable. A massive train station went unused when the Americans were there, yet it remained

Waterfall in Dalat

impressive. Large churches and Buddhist temples were majestic, even though some were bullet laden and vacant. In the middle of town was the beautiful Xuan Huona Lake. I drove around this lake and a nearby waterfall when getting fuel for my ¾ ton truck at the gas depot near the Cam Ly Airport. Except for the signal sites in and around Dalat, including Pr'Line, the military had no need and were not invited to be in Dalat.

Less frequently, we traveled to Cam Ranh. This is where we picked up Tropo supplies. These trips included at least an overnight stay, and sometimes we were there for two or three days per visit. While in Cam Ranh, we would enjoy the white beaches and clear water of the South China Sea. There, we could obtain snorkeling equipment, fishing equipment and underwater spears.

Once Mike and I ventured out far from the beach while diving under the surface and trying to spear fish in the crys-

Sunrise over Cam Ranh Bay

tal-clear water. Our quest was cut short, however, when we saw bullets streaking through the water not far from us. We did our swimming "personal best" rushing to get out of the water. When on the beach, an army guard approached and informed us that the shots were his attempts to warn us that we were approaching a dangerous rip tide current. The guard's actions were benign, if not benevolent, yet it didn't feel that way at the moment. Apart from this incident, most journeys to Cam Ranh were mini-R&R's.

Most of us on the hill attempted to bolster our creativity. We would write home to our loved ones, write poetry and practice amateur photography. In the evenings and during downtime, Mike provided background music with his acoustic guitar. His mellow finger picking improved through the year, and for Marc and me, we had a peaceful soundtrack to the war.

After being in country for about eight months, I was awarded a five-day vacation back to the states. I had already taken my R&R in Hawaii where I spent a wonderful and blessed week with my wife. We totally toured the Oahu island. We took in the International Marketplace, the Don Ho show, Pearl Harbor, Diamond Head and Waikiki Beach. However, this vacation break was different. I was to spend five days in my home in Missouri. I reunited with my wife, my parents, siblings, extended family and friends.

Now to the point of this story. As I packed my duffel bag and gathered the muster to return to Nam for four more months, I decided to bring along my tenor saxophone. Could I also add melody to the melancholia? Mike certainly did.

Well, as it turned out, Mike and I were able to blend our friendship with music. We mastered a dozen or so tunes and determined we would share our talent with others.

Our Chaplain, Captain Gorham, arranged for us to "perform" at GI organized churches on LBM, in Cam Ranh Bay and a Baptist missionary complex in Dalat.

We traveled in a jeep with a white cross painted on the front. I'm not sure if the VC or NVA honored the message implied with the cross, but at the time, we believed they did. Mike tells the story of seeing a group of Vietnamese, while driving through a small town, that were wearing the "black pajamas" uniforms and carrying AK-47s. We zipped through this hamlet feeling more curious then fearful. When we traveled with the Chaplain, we felt secure and protected. In retrospect, we also, as usual, possessed a significant portion of denial.

These "gigs" to churches and religious services offered Mike and me a diverse education to our religious naiveté. Mike was a Roman Catholic and I was a traditional Protestant. What we experienced at some of the services involved "freestyle" activities with which we were unfamiliar.

At any rate, we appreciated the diverse ways that some embraced music and expressed their faith. These adventures certainly solved our issues of boredom. Beyond this, these outings fed our spirits and enriched our lives.

During our time that remained, Mike and I would often break into a therapeutic jam session. The times of "making music" were probably of little interest to our other brothers on the hill, but for Mike and me, it was more than just a pastime; it was the source of great bonding.

Each convoy and adventure was like climbing a mountain or landing an airplane. These were times when the adrenaline ran high and the focus became acute. I wonder now if the rush experienced in convoy travel and other risky activities, was to feel alive in the shadows of the fear of death.

Men of Tropo filling sandbags

Mai the monkey looking for a treat in the author's pocket

6

DEPARTURE

~OVERCOMING DARKNESS~

We perch on a world of beauty and might,
Brilliant spheres among us, and the absence of light.
Human nature, like the natural earth,
Has benevolent waves where shadows give birth.

Can one plunge beyond another's reach?
Humanum est errare – yes.
Might one fully measure the repercussions of a kindness?
Likely not.

So, what are the prerequisites of redemption per se?
Strengthen my talk in a certain way?
Need I a cape, a walking line?
Fancy a mask to hide behind?

Does the desire of intent realize resolve?
De bonne grace – yes.
Will the absence of understanding retard
the completion of wholeness?
Possibly not.

Darkness among us and selfish deeds
Are overcome when oneness proceeds.
We are one with all nature, and this singularity, it would seem,
Is a universal formula to be and redeem. (RLM)

* * * *

FOR ME, ON THE day I was supposed to begin my processing out of country, getting off the hill was no small feat. Viet Cong activity had picked up in the last several days and "routine" travel was curtailed. Typically, we could call for a ride to Cam Ranh (or wherever we needed to go), and a chopper would pick us up at our heliport. If we needed to go somewhere, chances were a helicopter was headed in that direction, and we could call for one like calling for a taxi. Our heliport, which was approximately a twenty-foot square spot and visually identified with a smoke grenade, was amusingly named "The Pr'Line International Airport."

However, on this day, August 29, 1971, our area was considered too "hot" for workaday travel. Only two days left "in country" and I was to go home! Return to the world! I learned a few days earlier when my "orders" arrived, that I was to be dismissed from the service when I returned to Fort Lewis, Washington. My remaining three months of active duty was being waived, and I was about to be a civilian. I was packed and ready to go but couldn't get off the hill!

Finally, a pilot radioed back. "I will be going over Pr'Line in thirty minutes. I will hover for you to jump on board but will not touch ground as the area is too hot."

The chopper approached at a much faster speed than I had ever seen before. I threw my bags on, and the gunner extended his hand and pulled me in. I was sitting on the floor of the Huey when the gunner locked a strap in front of me, and up we shot. My camera was dangling around my neck, and I grabbed it for a picture. My last photo of

Pr'Line captured my boots hanging out of the open door of the chopper as we sped away.

The night before, the V.C. had blown up an ammunition dump in Cam Ranh. The blast had destroyed several buildings and many were still burning. *My soul*, I thought, *this place looks like Hades!*

Being "short" was the term given to a soldier that had little time remaining in Nam. I was so short; I could hardly see out when I learned that I was to be an extra day in "short" status. I had counted the days. Typically, a tour of duty was 365 days. My 366th day was a long day for sure. All domestic flights, both in and out of Cam Ranh, were stopped. Yet the "processing out" on August 31, went smoothly. No delays because of health, no drugs in my urine test, no contraband that was sniffed out by dogs.

The author hanging out of a Huey helicopter as he departed Pr'Line for the last time

We were allowed to board our freedom bird. My friend
Marc had a more complicated departure.

> **Bourque:** *When I received word that my tour of*
> *duty was over and I was to go home, I was filled*
> *with many emotions. Elation, of course! I also felt*
> *the grief of separation from the men I worked with*
> *on the hill that had become my brothers. Brothers*
> *who shared memories of our bonds and some ex-*
> *periences we didn't want to remember. Yet ex-*
> *citement was building with the fact that I was*
> *going home! Very shortly I would be with my*
> *family and friends in the country that I loved. I*
> *had made it! I was going home and I was proud to*
> *be an American, proud to be a soldier.*
>
> *All of my dreams and pride started to shatter,*
> *however, as things started to fall apart during my*
> *"out of country" processing. I had to take a urinal-*
> *ysis test for drug use like everyone else. My results*
> *came back positive. I had never, ever, used drugs!*
> *I was pulled out of line as we were waiting to*
> *board the bus that took us to the plane for the long*
> *ride home. When I was finally allowed to come*
> *home, which was several days after my original*
> *plan date, I arrived in the states as an unknown. I*
> *was not listed on any arrival roster and there was*
> *no information as to where my next duty assign-*
> *ment was to be. I felt like a man without a country.*
> *At this point, in November, I was finally given*
> *tickets to go home, to Maine. I was instructed that*
> *my orders would be sent to me in a few weeks.*

Two months later, in January, orders came for me to be stationed in Fort Huachuca, Arizona. I arrived at Fort Huachuca with the rank of E-4. The following August I ran into a former brother who served with me on Pr'Line Mountain. We were supposed to be on the same flight home, but as I stated earlier, I was held back. Randy asked me what happened, and why I was still an E-4 when I was on the same promotion orders that he was on. Randy was now an E-5 and explained that we were to be automatically promoted when we came back from Vietnam.

Since my name was on his copy of his promotion, I was able to go to the comptroller and argue my case that I should have been promoted to an E-5 the previous November. After a lot of persuading, the Army eventually found my promotion papers in the history section of my personnel file. Finally, I was given my promotion to E-5 with nine and a half months back pay. I am sure my case is not unique. I wonder how many more service men and women have had this happen, and the error was never corrected. Too often, and on many levels, things could and did go wrong. To use our author's words, "sometimes it was overcast, sometimes we were in the clouds." Because of the intervention of my unit member and friend, Randy McFarland, I was promoted. Thank you, Randy, and may you rest in peace.

Silence.

Dead silence.

The jet engines began to roar, yet inside, silence remained.

As the plane lifted from the runway, as if choreographed and rehearsed, every man burst out with yells and screams. Some were laughing uncontrollably. Specifically, I do not remember what I said or the sounds I made. I do know that as I write this paragraph, tears are flowing. The sounds seemed to vibrate the entire cabin. This, I was to appreciate later, was true catharsis. This was all to be repeated when the captain announced that we had just crossed into International waters. Again, one more time, when we landed in Washington.

7

STIGMA

~MAZE~

The sun danced on the clouds blow.
Ominous turbulence under the surface
Concealed the gates of Hell.

One end of a rainbow stretched to the south –
Bursting with color.
The other end was ablaze with darkness.

We are who we are because of where we've been.
Some journeys accompany strain and pain.
These are the treks that generate gain.

Prayers accompanied many of the journeys.
The Way, the Truth, and the Life.
Amazing life – sacred maze. (RLM)

* * * *

THE WAR IN VIETNAM created intense feelings on the home front and in Southeast Asia. It became increasingly clear that the American presence in South Vietnam was not accomplishing the original goal, whatever that was. The riots throughout the United States were becoming fatal. Progressively, the U.S. soldiers were asking, "what are we doing here?" It seemed that most of us in Tropo in 1970/71 simply felt like it was a part of our patriotic duty. I remember thinking that my dad was probably not particularly fond of being stationed in the Philippines during World War II either.

For some, however, such was not the case. In the United States, young men were burning their draft cards, and riots were raging in our cities. I have a granddaughter in her second year at Kent State – a far calmer place now than it was then. For the Americans in Southeast Asia, many began to fight the military officers with tactics similar to what was used against the NVA and the VC. In the states, the antiwar movement was in the open and on the news. The revolt among the American soldiers was not so public. The Tet Offensive seemed to be the turning point of the Vietnam war. We could win the battles but didn't seem to be winning the war. Those in the military and those in civilian life began to hear stories of military leaders being killed with "friendly fire."

"Fragging" became the slang for the execution of officers. The word is derived from fragmentation grenade. Fragging was the weapon that tended to cover up the evidence. It was believed that many American officers killed in the war were killed by enlisted men.

Unfortunately, Pr'Line was not exempt from these threats. Early in 1970, there were four enlisted men that were killed while two of them were constructing a bomb, believed to be intended for an officer.

This action, along with many threats, caused as much

fear among officers as did "Charlie." This was somewhat true with enlisted men turning on enlisted men as well as officers. In many ways, parts of Vietnam were like the wild, wild west. It was not good for one to have an enemy. Blurred clarity made it difficult to determine who all were the enemy. It was cloudy!

With the war dragging on way beyond tolerance level, the public begin to associate the disdain of the war with the American soldiers. Massacres like what happened in My Lai added to this contempt. Since I was discharged from the army immediately upon my return from Vietnam, I avoided the discrimination and assaults that many did not.

> **Bourque**: *When I got back to the States in November, 1971, I was unprepared for the inhumane treatment I received. During my processing, I was advised by those doing my processing that since I was traveling to the northeast, it was unsafe for me to travel in uniform. I was led to a separate room and told that I could put on some civilian clothes where I could travel home safely. When I finally reached home, I had to explain to my parents why I was in civilian clothes and not my uniform. They had a hard time understanding these reasons, and by the looks they gave me, I felt that they were somewhat disappointed in me. Yet, I was home and it felt good to be back in the good old USA.*
>
> *That positive emotion of being home quickly faded, however, after gathering with some of my high school classmates and close friends. These "friends" started referring to me as the Vietnam baby killer. Those*

words really hurt. I was in the Signal Corps, and I never shot my weapon at anybody at any time. Needless to say, I put a lot of distance between myself and my so-called friends. This was also the beginning of my putting aside my Vietnam memories. I acted like I never went to Nam. I seldom talked about my tour of duty to anyone. At times I felt ashamed that I was a Vietnam veteran.

Weir: I have one memory that I have tried hard to forget. It was my return flight to the States. I'm sure we all remember the sheer joy when the plane lifted off the runway when leaving Nam and a second wave of joy when we touched down in the States. My flights had those same joys but then something went terribly wrong.

When our plane landed, instead of going to the gate, the plane stopped on the apron. We thought we were just waiting to get an available gate, but then the pilot came on the intercom and told us we were being diverted to the furthest point away from the terminal because of a "threat" made on our arrival! Imagine our confusion/fear. We survived a year in Vietnam and now our own citizens wanted to kill us? After what seemed like an eternity, the plane was searched. When nothing was found, we returned to the terminal.

I've tried to forget this memory, because the whole experience was one that I could not understand. It wasn't one of my fondest memories, and one I've tried hard to forget. Try as I did, I still remember this!

I was never called a baby killer or treated accordingly. Yet, by some means, I learned to not refer to my being a Vietnam veteran. It wasn't until after 9/11/2001, that I started to stand at events where veterans were asked to stand. It was also after 9/11 that I heard the words, "Thank you for your service." Thirty years after my service, I heard the words, "Welcome home."

At first after returning home, I wanted to share my pictures, primarily with my family. I brought back 1,000 slides of my travels in Vietnam. I tried to capture the things I saw and the places I had been. My camera hung around my neck almost all the time, especially on my journeys off the hill. However, it seemed that no one was interested in seeing them. The pictures opened wounds that no one seemed to understand, much less articulate. I did not appreciate until years later, that Vietnam created pain for my family too. All of our wounds were different, but we were all wounded. We seemed to find solace in denial and ignoring the subject. We were fairly successful with our attempts to forget.

8

REUNION

~GROWTH~

I now believe that this full tour
has been pivotal for all.
Gestures of sacrifice and empathic care
can never be considered small.
Forfeiture is a legion of things
good, bad, curb and disturb.
A peculiar potion we sometimes drink
when enlightenment awaits superb.
The year brought monsoons and clammy sun
wet tears remained awhile.
Innocence was lost as maturity gained
and growth caused enduring smiles. (RLM)

* * * *

SINCE MY TROPO BROTHERS have been reuniting (in person, on the phone, through email and text, and by zoom), I think about Vietnam every day. Some days are filled with remembering experiences, emotions and my newly found, old – old friends. I would have been able to identify some of my brothers in a "line up." Others have changed beyond the quick recognition. We seem to have all acquired a facial patina.

Yet, it is mystical that for the first time in my life, I am simultaneously seeing these brothers both as they were and as they are. How they looked and how they look. Interestingly, the fundamental personality of each seems unchanged. Further, the fifty years have not changed how we sound. Our speech patterns and accents have remained.

At a recent zoom, we talked at length how fortunate we were that, if we had to go to Vietnam, Pr'Line mountain was the place to be. The mountain top did not have the searing heat that was present in most of the country. Our nights were cool. Like the rest of the country, we had two seasons, wet and dry, yet, our temperatures were comfortable. Being perched above the jungle as we were, gave us a bird's eye view.

The men of Tropo all seemed to have pleasant dispositions. We had all gone through the highly specialized training at Ft. Monmouth and this unique MOS added to our bonding. Oh, I guess we had our days, but we were brothers. Our bonds were greater than existed in many families. Most military companies could not make this claim.

Care and compassion went far beyond Tropo. Don Bosco, the Catholic orphanage in Phat Chi, and the Baptist Missionary Complex in Dalat were perfect examples of compassionate care. Further, kindness of people in Phat Chi extended far beyond our momasan.

Then there was, and is, the beautiful city of Dalat with its terraced fields, beautiful architecture, tranquil lakes and inspiring waterfalls. We felt fortunate. To be sure, similar to the "Yellow Brick Road," we had to be on the lookout for dangerous animals – including "Charley."

This vet had no choice but to be in the Army, I was drafted. There was no choice about going to Vietnam. Nor was there a choice about being assigned to Pr'Line in the Central Highlands. Be that as it may, I and most of us in Tropo felt (and still feel) fortunate to have landed where we did.

Weir*: I successfully blocked out Nam for nearly fifty years. Perhaps it's just the number of years or maybe it was one too many PBRs. When Ken called me, it rattled my cage. I started looking at pictures and albums that I hadn't looked at for half a century. As I reflected, it was the experiences that I wanted to forget and not the ones with whom I served. When I had the chance to get together with these guys, I had to do it.*

As we reconnected at our reunion last year, I learned that many things have escaped my memory. I cannot remember basic things like my room, my roommates, the mess hall or even where we worked. Some incidents stand out like when Dave Fry was injured, and when we were ambushed in Claymore Alley. I remember guard duty on New Year's Eve but even these events have no details for me.

What I do remember, fondly, are the people. When we chat on zoom, I don't see a seventy-one-year-old man, I see the face of the twenty-one-year-old! We've talked about the pizza parties, the holidays (and the parties) and playing basketball. These are the memories I want to remember.

So maybe the many PBRs did their job, because I

*don't remember as much of the bad times as I do of
the happier ones.*

Our memories unite us with the past, yet, in some surprising ways, these memories are acquiring a sense of freshness. It's more for me than just remembering what I forgot. It's remembering more clearly what I remembered. Part of this is because I have recently been straining to remember. For years I intentionally and unconsciously worked to forget. This was reinforced by our cultural stigma. Now I want to remember everything – the good and the bad, the beautiful and the ugly. There seems a paradox that I struggled to forget what I now strain to remember.

Another reason memories are being resurrected is because of the conversations that are occurring among my old friends. With selected experiences, we have reconstructed memories in orchestrated unison. Like synchronized swimmers, our memories have become greater than the sum of our individual parts.

"Oh yes," we would alternately say, "I remember that too."

"Do you remember how much changed while we were in Nam?"

"Oh My! I remember that Johnny Carson had black hair when I went to Nam, and his hair was white when I returned."

"I remember that women's skirts were below the knee when I left and were mini when I got back."

"And bras were an option!"

In the late 1960s and early '70s, the guys of Tropo were techno geeks. I could, and did, patch a signal from our communication van to "Long Lines" (on the hill). From there I got a signal to the Philippines. From the Philippines, I could usually find a Ham Radio operator in Guam and/or Hawaii. Once I got this far, I could reach Ma Bell on the west coast and give the family phone number to the operator. Since we had at least one patch through a Ham Radio operator, we had to say "Over" when our communication was alternating back and forth. Then the Ham Radio operator could switch from transmit to receive. When recounting this story at one of our reunions, Ken said, "I did this a few times myself."

"Hey," Marc said, "you didn't let me in on this secret!"

Now, well let's say, we all feel "behind the 8 ball" when it comes to technology. So much has changed over the last fifty years, it's hard to fathom.

People were not very interested in the moon missions when we returned to the states. Why not I wondered! Since then, the Space Shuttle program has come and gone. Now civilians are buying seats on missions to outer space. Recording devices have moved from tapes, to CD's, to digital. We now all have personal computers, use the internet, access the World Wide Web and Google what we want to know (certainly not with the ease of our children and grandchildren). We use GPS (oh how useful this would have been in Nam), caller ID, Facebook, YouTube and computer gaming (remember the Commodore 64?). TVs are now flat screens that hang on the wall! Today we can access our homes and cars with digital codes and voice commands. Many of us now have Hybrid cars that are capable of parallel parking and have no need for a spare tire. Planes do not need a pilot and soon our cars won't need a driver. Smart phones now consolidate most of the technology that has presented in the last several decades. Our cell phones are now likely more powerful that the massive Philco Ford computer that was at Crypto when we were at Fort Monmouth. We were amazed at the changes we experienced when returning from Vietnam, and we are even more amazed at the changes that have occurred in our lifetimes. I now appreciate that my father must have felt similarly after returning from WWII.

One of our greatest tools to help restore memories of our Vietnam experiences are our pictures. Since reuniting, we have expanded our picture gallery by sharing meaningful photos. Many memories have become unstuck through this visualization process.

This vet brought back ten trays of slides. Each tray had 100 slots for the slides. Experiences of people and places that I captured on film assisted the memories I have retained. One thousand photos I brought back! What if I would have returned with 2000 slides? Would I have an expanded memory? Would my memory be more precise?

Perhaps the greatest reason our collective memories are now so important and indeed improving, is because we are now visiting these memories with fifty years of expanded wisdom. These recollections are now not only of a twenty-one or twenty-two-year-old, there is now an angle offered by a seventy-one or seventy-two year-old. Just imagine what we didn't know then that we do know now. It may be good that what we now know was inaccessible back then.

Oh, how we stressed to forget what we now anxiously try to remember! When we left Vietnam, we became disengaged, divided by circumstances and dismembered. Now after we have reconnected, we are engaged, united in spirit and remembered!

August 2021 snapshot of Tropo zoom. *Top L to R:* Mike and Rosie Brogan, Ken and Janice Ottens, Marc and Pat Bourque, Robert and Ruth Menz. *Middle L to R:* Daryl Gardner, Jim Singleterry, Jim Thomas, Lenny Weir. *Bottom L to R:* Jerry and Dee Sharp, Mike Penners

ABOUT THE AUTHOR

R OBERT L. MENZ, DMin, served with the Tropo brotherhood on Pr'Line Mountain, Vietnam, from September,
1970, to September, 1971. Menz is a retired Certified Em-
ployee Assistance Professional, Educator, and Pastoral Psy-
chotherapist. He is the author of *A Memoir of a Pastoral
Counseling Practice* and *A Pastoral Counselors Model for
Wellness in the Workplace: Psychergonomics*, both from
Haworth press. He is the editor/author of *Changing Soci-
ety: A Social and Spiritual Vision for the Year 2020 and
Beyond* from University Press of America. In addition,
Menz authored *Divine Entreaty: Prayers for Public and
Diverse Settings* and *Theo: The Circle of a Transcendent*
both from Balboa Press, and is a contributing author to
*Departures 2010: Writings by the Faculty, Staff, Alumni,
& Students of Edison Community College* – as well as
numerous articles in professional journals. In 2017, Menz

was selected for the Marquis Who's Who Lifetime Achievement award. He and his wife Ruth together have four children and six grandchildren. They live in Sidney, Ohio, and enjoy traveling and communing with nature.

www.hellgatepress.com

Made in the USA
Las Vegas, NV
17 February 2022

44107738R00066